MW00674382

# THE GOD THAT COMES NEAR

a study on the book of Haggai

*by*
KRISTIN SCHMUCKER

table of
# CONTENTS

# Study Suggestions

Thank you for choosing this study to help you dig into God's Word. We are so passionate about women getting into Scripture, and we are praying that this study will be a tool to help you do that. Here are a few tips to help you get the most from this study:

• Before you begin, take time to look into the context of the book. Find out who wrote it and learn about the cultural climate it was written in, as well as where it fits on the biblical timeline. Then take time to read through the entire book of the Bible we are studying if you are able. This will help you to get the big picture of the book and will aid in comprehension, interpretation, and application.

• Start your study time with prayer. Ask God to help you understand what you are reading and allow it to transform you (Psalm 119:18).

• Look into the context of the book as well as the specific passage.

• Before reading what is written in the study, read the assigned passage! Repetitive reading is one of the best ways to study God's Word. Read it several times, if you are able, before going on to the study. Read in several translations if you find it helpful.

• As you read the text, mark down observations and questions. Write down things that stand out to you, things that you notice, or things that you don't understand. Look up important words in a dictionary or interlinear Bible.

• Look for things like verbs, commands, and references to God. Notice key terms and themes throughout the passage.

• After you have worked through the text, read what is written in the study. Take time to look up any cross-references mentioned as you study.

• Then work through the questions provided in the book. Read and answer them prayerfully.

• Paraphrase or summarize the passage, or even just one verse from the passage. Putting it into your own words helps you to slow down and think through every word.

• Focus your heart on the character of God that you have seen in this passage. What do you learn about God from the passage you have studied? Adore Him and praise Him for who He is.

• Think and pray through application and how this passage should change you. Get specific with yourself. Resist the urge to apply the passage to others. Do you have sin to confess? How should this passage impact your attitude toward people or circumstances? Does the passage command you to do something? Do you need to trust Him for something in your life? How does the truth of the gospel impact your everyday life?

• We recommend you have a Bible, pen, highlighters, and journal as you work through this study. We recommend that ballpoint pens instead of gel pens be used in the study book to prevent smearing. Here are several other optional resources that you may find helpful as you study:

• www.blueletterbible.org This free website is a great resource for digging deeper. You can find translation comparison, an interlinear option to look at words in the original languages, Bible dictionaries, and even commentary.

• A Dictionary. If looking up words in the Hebrew and Greek feels intimidating, look up words in English. Often times we assume we know the meaning of a word, but looking it up and seeing its definition can help us understand a passage better.

• A double-spaced copy of the text. You can use a website like www.biblegateway.com to copy the text of a passage and print out a double-spaced copy to be able to mark on easily. Circle, underline, highlight, draw arrows, and mark in any way you would like to help you dig deeper and work through a passage.

DAY ONE

WEEK ONE

# Read
## THE ENTIRE BOOK OF HAGGAI

*After reading the entire book of Haggai, what key words and themes stand out to you?*

_____

*What verse stuck out to you the most?*

_____

*Write out a prayer asking God to show you more of who He is through the book of Haggai.*

_____

# WEEK ONE

# Introduction
## TO HAGGAI

*Read the entire book of Haggai*

Most of us probably haven't read Haggai in long time. And finding this short book may require a trip to the table of contents at the front of our Bibles. And yet tucked in this short book of only thirty-eight verses is truth that teaches us who God is and how we should live in light of that truth. Haggai is the Word of God, and the Word of God is for us.

The book of Haggai is found at the end of the Old Testament. This short book does in fact take place at the end of the Old Testament timeline. The events inside the book are widely accepted to have taken place in 520 BC as a small remnant returns back to Jerusalem after the exile. We don't know much about the book's author, but we do know that his name was Haggai and he was a prophet that spoke the Word of the Lord. We see his longing and pleading to the people to focus their lives on what mattered: the Lord.

As we begin to think about the book of Haggai, it is helpful for us to think about what has happened in the Old Testament up until this point. Scripture began in Genesis 1 as God made the world and everything in it. But by Genesis 3, sin enters the world at the fall. Though the consequence of Adam and Eve's sin in the garden was death, God made a promise that a Redeemer would come. They didn't know when or how, but God promised them that day that His plan that was set before the ages began would come to pass. In Genesis 12, we are introduced to a man named Abraham, and God makes a covenant with him and promises him that the Messiah would come from his line and that all nations would find blessing in his seed. Eventually, the people of Israel would be enslaved in Israel, but God would faithfully deliver them and make a covenant with Moses. There were promises of blessing for obedience and consequences for disobedience (Genesis 19:3-6). When the people finally entered the promised land there were judges and kings that would lead them. And God made a covenant with one king in particular. To David, God promised that a king would come through David's line that would sit on the throne forever (2 Samuel 7:8-16). God's faithfulness to His people is present on every page of the Old Testament. Sadly, we cannot say the same for the people. Despite God's steadfast love and faithfulness, the people rebelled against His gracious hand (2 Kings 17:5-15), and the people would be sent into captivity as a result of their sin (2 Chronicles 36:15-20). The nation that had been promised blessing and God's very presence had chosen exile instead. But still, God was faithful. He promised that a remnant would return and that the promise of the coming Messiah would still come about.

We pick up in the book of Haggai at the end of that long exile and captivity. God had promised that a remnant would return, and Haggai would be a prophet to this returned remnant. After years in exile, the people returned in 538 BC. The book of Haggai may be small, but it is packed with a big message to the remnant that returned. The people had become apathetic and were seeking after material wealth and success. While many of the Minor Prophets focus on the people's lack of justice to the oppressed, Haggai focuses on how the people's excess, misplaced priorities, and sin had led them to demonstrate a lack of justice toward God Himself. The people were not giving God what He deserved. Haggai calls them to look to God. He calls them to rebuild the temple. He calls them to take their focus off of themselves and to fix their gaze on the Covenant God.

The book of Haggai is a call not only to put God first, but to keep Him central to every part of life.

There are many themes in the book of Haggai. Though this book consists of just two chapters and 38 verses, it is overflowing with a message for the people of Haggai's day, and a message that we can learn so much from as well. The book instills in us the matchless worth of the Word of the Lord. Over and over we see that phrase in the book. God's Word is what changes us, and that is just as true for us today as it was for those in Haggai's day. Other themes include the temple, the apathy of the people, God's covenant faithfulness, and God's sovereignty. There is also a great emphasis on both messianic hope and the future consummation and restoration of all things – when God makes all things new. Throughout the book, we see three

key people, Haggai, Joshua, and Zerubbabel. In them, we see the roles of prophet, priest, and king displayed. And ultimately, we are pointed to Jesus who is our great prophet, priest, and king.

The book of Haggai is a call to worship. And it is also a reminder that God has not forgotten His promises. He is faithful and now He calls His people to be faithful.

*How does the context of the book of Haggai in the story of Scripture help you to understand its message?*

_____

*Write a summary of the message of Haggai.*

_____

*Why do you think we need to hear the message of Haggai today?*

_____

DAY THREE

WEEK ONE

# Haggai 1:1-2

## THE WORD OF THE LORD

The first verses of Haggai give us insight into the context and necessity of the book. The book opens with the remnant that has returned on the first day of the sixth month. This is equivalent to the start of August and would have been the time of the fruit harvest in the land. It was also the time of the monthly offerings that had been commanded in Numbers 28:11-15. Yet the temple had not been rebuilt after the exile.

We are introduced to the prophet Haggai. It is clear from both the books of Haggai and Ezra that Haggai was a prophet (Haggai 1:1,3,12,2:1, Ezra 5:1, 6:14). The Old Testament prophet followed in the footsteps of Moses and was the mouthpiece of God to the people. The prophet is the one that God used to deliver His Word to His people which is why we see the prophets frequently using language like, "Thus says the Lord." We find this prophetic address in the book of Haggai and we also find the phrase, "The word of the LORD came," repeated throughout the text. It was God's words to the people that came through Haggai. God was speaking a specific message at a specific time to a specific people. We will look at what these words meant for the people of Judah in Haggai's day, and then we will also consider the transcendent and eternal message that God is speaking to us through the prophet.

It is God's Word that does the work. Haggai was a prophet, but he had no special ability other than a calling by God to be the mouthpiece of God and to proclaim the message of God to the people. God still works through His Word, and He has called us to faithfully proclaim the Word of the gospel. Haggai stands out among the prophets. While most see a prophet speak to an unrepentant people, in the book of Haggai we see the people repent and obey. We can learn from the faithfulness of the prophets. They proclaimed the message no matter what the outcome was. And we are called to do the same.

Throughout the book, Haggai will use the name "The LORD of Hosts." This is one of the most popular designations of God in the prophets, and it is seen often in the post-exilic prophets (Haggai, Zechariah, Malachi). This name combines Yahweh which is the covenant name of God designated in English by the all capital LORD with a descriptor that signifies the almighty, sovereign control of God. This reminds us that God is the commander of the angel armies and hold all power and authority on earth. He is in control.

The Word of the Lord comes first to the leaders of the people. We are introduced to Zerubbabel who is the governor of Judah, and Joshua who is the high priest. Though the people had been in the land for over 16 years, the temple had not been rebuilt. The work had been begun as seen in the first chapters of Ezra, but it had been abandoned when opposition came from the Samaritans. The word of the Lord declares that the people thought that it was not yet time to rebuild the house of the Lord. The book reminds us that delayed obedience is not obedience.

God had been the one to bring the remnant back (Ezra 1:1). Yet despite His faithfulness, the people had been sidetracked by opposition that left them paralyzed. They came into the land and they built their houses and established the economy. The people failed to realize that greatest devastation of the exile was not the people being carried away into captivity or even the destruction of the city and the temple. The most heartbreaking part of the exile was that the glory of God had departed. The people knew that the temple needed to be rebuilt so that God could be worshipped in holiness, but they didn't think it was quite time to do it. They thought there were more important things to be done, and in doing so they forfeited the presence of God.

The tiny book of Haggai contains eternal truth about who God is and how He desires to be worshipped. We too, like the people of Judah, are prone to get distracted by opposition. We are tempted to focus on building our own lives and thinking that we will get around to serving the Lord eventually. But Haggai calls us to something better. Haggai reminds us that God speaks through His Word. If God is speaking to you, don't delay your obedience (Psalm 95:7-8). The book reminds us that life doesn't always go as planned and opposition comes, but the detours of life should never stop us from worshipping. Above all we learn that we should desire the presence and glory of God more than anything.

*Why would it be important for the people to know that what Haggai was saying was the word of the Lord?*

_____

*Why do we need God's Word?*

_____

*The people planned to obey, but they never got around to it. However, delayed obedience is not obedience. In what ways have you been tempted to delay obedience in your own life?*

_____

# WEEK ONE

# Haggai 1:3-6
## CONSIDER YOUR WAYS

Consider your ways. This is the call that Haggai brings by the word of the Lord. The people were claiming that it wasn't yet time to rebuild the temple, and God speaks strong words in response to this. The people are dwelling in their finished houses while God's house is a pile of dust and rubble. When the people say that it is not yet time, God's response is to point out the situation and ask if this is what it is time for. God has no dwelling place and worship has been forsaken while His people go on as if nothing is wrong.

God calls them to consider their ways. To think deeply about their condition. He calls them to self-examination. A long hard look at what was happening reveals the idols that have formed in their hearts. They had been rescued from the exile by the Lord and they were far away from the foreign idols, and yet idols had begun to form in their hearts. The human heart in its natural state is what John Calvin called idol factories. The people had been no stranger to falling into the sin of worshipping physical idols that had been made with hands, but on many other occasions they worshipped idols of their own imaginations. They formed in their minds a picture of who God was, instead of living in light of the Word of God. The work of the temple's rebuilding had been abandoned because of the opposition on the outside, and it continued to be abandoned because of the sin in their hearts. Their personal comfort had taken precedence over worship.

A closer look at the people's situation proves that it wasn't as good as it seemed. They lived in their paneled house, but peace and contentment were nowhere to be found. They were living in their own strength and doing their own thing and it wasn't working out as great as they had planned. Throughout the Old Testament we are reminded of the blessings that come from covenant faithfulness and the consequences that come from covenant disobedience (Deuteronomy 28, Leviticus 26). The people were experiencing these covenant consequences, but it seems they didn't even notice. Their life was full of struggle and discontentment and yet they didn't realize that it was a consequence of their own unfaithfulness.

They were spinning their wheels and failing to realize what they had done. This is what makes the command to consider their ways so profound. It seems that they had neglected to do it before. They kept going through the motions without realizing that their sin had placed a wedge between them and the Lord (Isaiah 59:2). The phrase that is translated as "consider your ways," is one that shows up several time in the book of Haggai. The people had to recognize that there was a problem with where they were. The people needed to repent. Repent and return is the ongoing theme of the prophetic books as a whole and the book of Haggai is no different. The people needed to repent, return, and be restored.

The thing is that perfect covenant faithfulness was never a possibility for this sin-stricken people. And this episode only further instills in us a reminder that is echoed throughout the pages of the Old Testament. We are incapable of keeping this law on our own. The people had all things, and yet they had no satisfaction. The people needed a Redeemer and so do we. This passage serves to point our hearts to the One who perfectly fulfilled the law in our place. It points us to Jesus. For those who have been redeemed, it reminds us that we cannot live in our own strength. We need Him for every single moment. And as we consider our ways, our sin, and our brokenness, we can also consider Jesus who has conquered death, sin, and hell so that we could be united to Him (Hebrews 12:2-3). Consider your ways, and then consider Him who is the answer.

What do we learn about God from this passage?

_____

Consider your ways. How can you better
walk in obedience to the Lord?

_____

Consider Jesus. How does the gospel enable
you to walk in obedience?

_____

# WEEK ONE

# Haggai 1:7-8
## FOR HIS GLORY

The Lord's call to "consider your ways" rings out again. However, this is not simply a call to build the temple, but a call to a heart change. God through Haggai is calling the people to stop thinking of God as an afterthought that is added on to all the other things that they must do. Instead, God is calling His people to be radically centered on His glory. He is calling us to the same.

This is a call to repentance. It is a call to an inward change of heart that is evidenced by an outward change of action. So the call to repentance also comes with a call to go up, to bring the wood, and to build God's house. It is not enough to think about the things that we need to change. We must, through the power of the Spirit in us, get up and do what God has called us to do. We must turn to God and by nature that means we must turn away from our sin.

So often we are tempted to stop short of full obedience. The delayed obedience of the people of Israel at the time of Haggai's prophecy is often times more similar to us than we would like to admit. The people recognized that the building of God's house was something that needed to be done, but they just didn't think that it was yet time to obey. The people had been discouraged and sidetracked by their enemies, and now they were discouraged and sidetracked by the building of their own lives. It is easy for us to recognize the things that God has called us to do, but it is often so much harder for us to get up and do them. Whether it is opening our Bibles and calling to God in prayer or fulfilling the call to go and make disciples, we often know what we are called to do and yet we fail to go and do it. But the book of Haggai reminds us that obedience looks like repentance for the ways we have failed to obey, and immediate action in obedience.

As God calls the people to action, He also gives them a purpose for their action. They are working for God's pleasure and glory. The people must repent for God's glory, respond for God's glory, and return to His covenant love for His glory.

The response of God's people in repentance and obedience brings great pleasure to God. And He is glorified through that obedience and worship. God desires worship. God had called His people out of Egypt and established them as a nation so that they might worship Him and that He might dwell with them. In the book of Exodus, God called the people to build the tabernacle to be the place where He would dwell and the place where they would worship. Throughout the Psalms we see calls to worship and glorify God. David desired to build a temple for the worship of God (2 Samuel 7). Here in Haggai, the people are being called to obey and to build the temple. Both of these would be acts of worship and would bring glory to God. God would be glorified in the obedience of His people, and that obedience would be a sacrifice of worship to Him. And when the temple was built, and His dwelling place was once again established they would worship again in His temple. Through obedience and through worship God would be glorified. This is what God

desires from His people. He is worthy of worship and deserving of all glory and honor.

This is our purpose as well. We live to bring Him glory. And everything we do should be done for His glory. We worship Him for who He is, and we glorify Him for all that He has done. We have no greater purpose for our lives than this.

*Has there ever been a time that you have been tempted to delayed obedience?*

_____

*What can you do this week to obey the Lord?*

_____

*List out a few aspects of the character of God that you can worship Him for today.*

_____

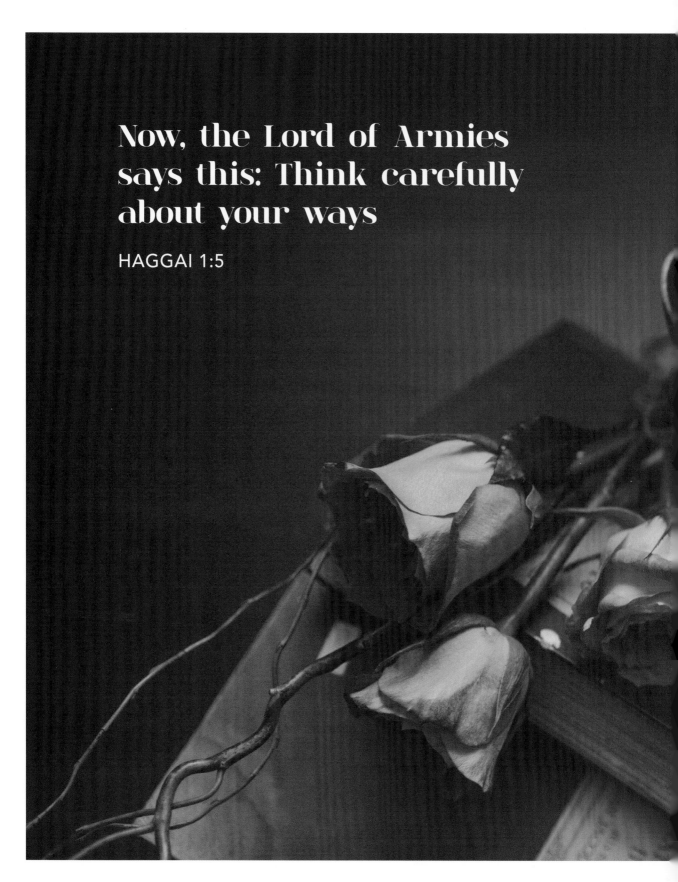

# Now, the Lord of Armies says this: Think carefully about your ways

HAGGAI 1:5

# WEEKLY REFLECTION
## Week One

## READ HAGGAI 1:1-8

*Paraphrase the passage from this week.*

_____

*What did you observe from this week's text about God and His character?*

_____

*What does the passage teach about the condition of mankind and about yourself?*

_____

*How does this passage point to the gospel?*

*How should you respond to this passage? What is the personal application?*

*What specific action steps can you take this week to apply the passage?*

WEEK TWO

# Haggai 1:9-11
## THE CONSEQUENCES OF APATHY

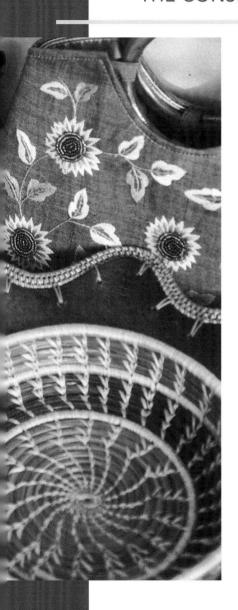

God pleads with the people to obey and bring Him glory and He also points out the consequences of their apathetic lives. In a very similar style as verses 3-6 we see that the people's efforts had been futile. The words should not be surprising to us when we think back on biblical history to this point. Deuteronomy 28 had been clear about the blessings of covenant faithfulness and the consequences for disobedience. The exile had been clear proof of God's faithfulness to fulfill that word and the consequences for disobedience had been clear. Yet somehow the people seem to miss that their situation was a direct result of their disobedience and apathetic hearts.

It is interesting to note that in the book of Haggai we do not see the striking calls of judgment or the woes against the injustice and idolatry of the people. The people in Haggai's day were not the overtly rebellious and idolatrous type – they simply thought that their own concerns were more important than the things of God. Though they had been delivered from the exile and were back in the promised land, they didn't seem to notice the great things that God had done for them that were right in front of them. They also didn't notice that their apathy and sin had led to judgment. God had sovereignly withheld from them the dew of the morning (Hosea 14:5), and the produce of the earth, and they didn't even realize that it was Him. While they built their houses and ignored the Lord's they did not even hear Him calling them to return.

Their apathetic hearts remind us of the church of Laodicea found in Revelation 3:14-22. They thought they had it all together without realizing that they were "wretched, pitiful, poor, blind, and naked." The call to the Laodiceans was the same. Jesus pleaded for repentance. Revelation 3:20 gives us a picture of Jesus standing at the door knocking. In context, this is far from a gentle knock and much more like Him pounding on the door and pleading for His church to wake up and see how they are living. The call is to repent and return just like it was in Haggai's day.

The call to build the Lord's temple was not as much about a building as it was about hearts that were fervent for God and totally devoted to Him. Throughout Scripture the temple is a symbol of the dwelling place of God. The dwelling place of God is seen from the opening pages of Scripture in Eden as God dwells with Adam and Eve, to the tabernacle (Exodus 25:8), to Jesus Himself coming to dwell among us (John 1:14), to the people of God where God dwells (1 Corinthians 3:16), and eventually in a new heaven and new earth where God will dwell in the midst of His people (Revelation 21-22). The dwelling place of God was a visual representation of transcendent spiritual realities. God longs to dwell with His people, but the people's hearts had wandered far from Him.

The truth of this book is enduring. It stands against the changes of time as it proclaims the unchanging character of our covenant God. Our hearts are prone to wander as well. We get wrapped up in our own little worlds and we think of our God and His work as an afterthought or something we will do when the time seems right. The words of the Lord through Haggai remind us to consider our ways and return to the Lord with repentant hearts for His glory and not our own.

*In what areas of your own life have you been tempted to focus on your own concerns instead of the things of God?*

_____

*Read today's passage again and list out the consequences of the people's disobedience and apathy.*

_____

*How should God's desire to dwell with His people reshape our thinking about our everyday lives?*

_____

DAY TWO

# WEEK TWO

# Haggai 1:12-15
## HEAR AND OBEY

The people heard the Word of God and then they obeyed. The message of Haggai had moved them to obedience. This short passage has much to teach us about what our response to the Word of God should be. Just as it did in the days of Haggai, the Word of God should compel us to obedience and to reverent worship as we are reminded of the character of our God.

The people repented and obeyed when they were confronted with their sin and this should be our response as well. Verse 12 also points out that the people feared the Lord. This fear is an awe, reverence, and submission to the Lord as the people saw His character. God's Word reveals who God is. That is exactly what it did for the remnant in Israel and it is what it does for us as well. As we see who God is, we are reminded that He is worthy of all worship and obedience. Our culture places a great emphasis on our need for self-awareness, but far more than we need self-awareness, we need God-awareness. And we cannot understand who we are without an understanding of who God is. An understanding of the character of God humbles us, encourages us, and compels us to worship and obey.

God's message to His people in verse 13 was a message of promise. In a declaration of covenant faithfulness, God reminded His people that He was with them. The message is found throughout Scripture and seen in Deuteronomy 31:6. God does not forget His people. The message that God is with His people is one of the most prominent themes in all of Scripture and it is encapsulated in one of the names given to Jesus. He is Emmanuel—God with us. This trust fills us with confident expectation and steadfast hope that even when our circumstances do not make sense, He has not left our side.

Obedience was the response of the people, but this obedience began in the leadership. Leaders are meant to lead and should always be the first to respond to the Word of God. This is a reminder for those in leadership to lead through submission to the Lord, and it is a reminder for all of us to pray for those that are leading us. All of us are leading someone and all of us are being led by someone, and we are called to lead through obedience to the Lord.

It was the Word of God that had the power to change the people, and it was the Spirit of God that stirred their hearts to respond. God stirred their hearts to follow and He gave them the power to do it. God was calling the people to rebuild His temple, but in the process, God was rebuilding the people. We are compelled to worship and to work not because of any goodness in ourselves, but because of God's working in us.

Isaiah 55 reminds us that the Word of God always accomplishes what God intends for it to do. Scripture never returns empty. There are many things that we can learn from this passage in Haggai. We must see our own need to obey and submit to the Word of God. We must be reminded that the Word of God exhorts us to the fear of God, and as we stand in awe of who He is we

obey. Above all, we must be reminded that our response to God is always just that – a response. We respond to who God is because of His work in us. We are enabled to obey by His Spirit that stirs our hearts. We are compelled to worship by His Word that reveals His character. It is the Lord that initiates, and we must simply respond through the strength that He alone provides.

Without His presence, the temple would have just been like any other building, but His presence changed everything. God no longer dwells in a temple, but in His people. The gospel proclaims to us that through the cross those that were once far off can be brought near to God (Ephesians 2:11-22). God once enabled the people to build a temple with literal stones, but now He is building His dwelling place with living stones (Ephesians 2:21-22, 1 Peter 2:1-10). God is building His church. The Word of God is still building the temple of God in His people and that is you and me.

Summarize what has happened in Haggai 1.

Why does the fear of the Lord compel
us to obedience and worship?

Read Isaiah 55. What does this passage tell
you about the character and Word of God?

Read Ephesians 2:11-22. What does this teach us
about how God is currently building His temple?

DAY THREE

# WEEK TWO

# Haggai 2:1-3
## THE GLORY DAYS

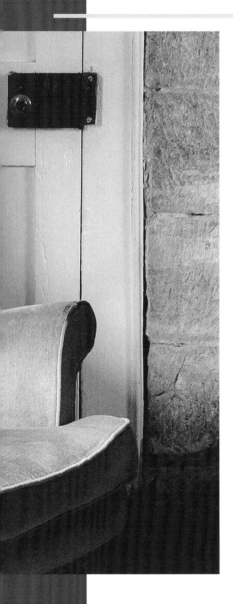

There is this tendency in all generations to talk about the glory days. We talk about days gone by with a nostalgic longing about how things once were. We reminisce about our childhoods and how things used to be. We talk about getting back to our roots and simpler times. Remembering our past is a good thing and God commands His people to do it often, and yet it is easy for us to slip from remembering God's faithfulness to coveting a past that never was. In today's passage, we will see a bit of both. We are reminded of the necessity of remembering and celebrating God's faithfulness in the past, and we are also reminded of the dangers of thinking that it just doesn't get any better than the good old days.

We may be tempted to skip over the first words of chapter two. The start of the first verse tells us the day on which the events took place, but if we rush by too quickly, we will fail to understand the deep significance of these words on this day. We are told that this message from the Lord through Haggai came in the seventh month on the twenty-first day. Though this likely means nothing to us, it was very significant. This was the last day of the feast of booths or tabernacles which was one of the most important feasts on the Jewish calendar. So this date should perk our attention in a similar way as if we were told that this took place on December 25th. The message comes just one month after the people had begun. They likely had not gotten very far and were probably getting discouraged at all the work that was ahead of them. On top of that, they would have just finished the feast of tabernacles or booths which meant that they would not have been working.

The feast of tabernacles was a time set forth to celebrate God's faithful provision for His people in the wilderness when they came out of Egypt. This specific feast celebrated how God had protected and provided for the people while they lived in the wilderness in tents. His presence had gone with them in a pillar of fire and a pillar of cloud and they lacked nothing. It was also at the time of this feast that the temple of Solomon had been dedicated generations before (1 Kings 8:1-3). How interesting that the people spent time remembering their own lack of a home in the wilderness at the time when God was calling them to rebuild His home. And how significant that the people would celebrate God's presence and provision through the Exodus as they themselves had just experienced a second exodus from the captivity of Babylon.

Later in the post-exilic period this feast would again bear great significance as the people in Nehemiah's day would have their hearts renewed for worship during this same feast (Nehemiah 8:13-18). Here in Haggai, the people that so long had neglected to be faithful to God were coming face to face with reminders of His steadfast faithfulness and love to them. With the people and the leaders gathered, Haggai again would speak the word of the Lord to the people. The people were likely discouraged, but it was far different than the apathy of chapter 1. The words of Haggai come not as a rebuke, but as an encouragement.

Haggai asks the people who had seen the house of God in its former glory. The people were discouraged. They were likely thinking and talking about how this new temple would never be like what it had been in the glory days of Solomon's temple. Instead of looking back and seeing God's faithfulness, they were looking back at what they thought would never be again. So Haggai's question to them is a rhetorical one as many of the prophets used. He is trying to teach them something important. They were looking back, when what they needed to do was to look forward. The glory days are not the days of years gone by. The glory days are every day as His glory shines before us. And the most glorious days are yet to come. For the people of God, the glory days are not in the past, but in the future. The glory days are the days when we will worship Him forever in His presence in the new heavens and the new earth. And just like the people in Haggai's day needed to be reminded to look forward, we do too.

*Why is it important for God's people to remember what God has done in the past?*

_____

*Why must we be careful not to idolize the past? How have you seen this happen?*

_____

*How are you encouraged in knowing that the glory days for the people of God are still ahead?*

_____

DAY FOUR

WEEK TWO

# Haggai 2:4-5
## THE PRESENCE OF THE LORD

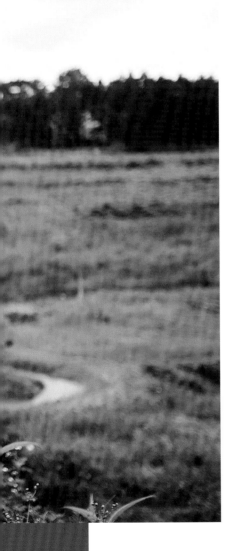

In the wake of the reminiscing of what the people perceived to be the glory days of Israel, and in continuation of Haggai's sermon on the final day of the Feast of Tabernacles, we pick up with two short verses that encourage our own hearts just as they must have encouraged their original audience.

Throughout the prophets, the message is repent and return. Here, Haggai does not stray from this formula, but he presents the same message as a message of hope. The message to repent and return is not merely one of judgment for past sin, it is one of hope for the future. And this is the message that Haggai proclaims. It is here that we see sin and grace held in tension, knowing that we cannot understand one fully without the other. We cannot know the weight and devastation of our sin, if we do not view it in light of God's perfect holiness and grace poured out for us. And we cannot know the glory of grace, if we do not first mourn the sin that made it necessary. And when we turn to God in repentance, our actions will follow in obedience. Obedience testifies to our repentance. And it is the knowledge of God that propels us to turn to the Lord. Here in the book of Haggai, the people looked at their situation and felt hopeless. But when their gaze was shifted to the person of God, they were strengthened for the work that was ahead of them.

And there would be work ahead of them. The encouragement from the Lord did not mean that there would not be work to do. But now in light of the word of God, the work ahead of them was filled with hope. What the people saw as the glory days of Israel was set in contrast to the glory and presence of God. Now they would see that though there was work to be done, it would be worth it.

The encouragement from God is hinged on the covenant promises of God and the reminder of when the people had been led out of Egypt by the Lord. Here we see the past set in its proper context. Not in a way that idolizes and idealizes the past, but in a way that declares the past faithfulness of God to be the source of hope for His present and future faithfulness. Instead of looking back and thinking that the past was better than the present, the people could remember the faithful and steadfast character of their covenant God, and be encouraged to trust Him for their future.

Three times in these two short verses, we see the command to be strong given to the people. Yet even this was not a new command. It would have been one that the people were intimately familiar with. It was the same command that has been given by Moses and by God Himself to Joshua in Deuteronomy 31:6-7 and Joshua 1:6,9. The words again would remind the people of how God had faithfully brought them into the land generations before.

The promise that accompanied this command to work was the presence of God. And it is God's presence and dwelling with His people that is one of the greatest themes of all of Scripture. God desires to dwell with His people. The theme is seen from the opening pages of Genesis as God walks with Adam and Eve in the garden, it is illustrated in God's presence in the tabernacle and temple, and it is manifested in Jesus who is Immanuel – God with us. Today it is seen in the indwelling Spirit of God in the church, and someday it will be fully realized and consummated in the new heavens and new earth where God will dwell in the midst of His people. In many ways, we can say that the presence of God among His people is the theme of the Bible. With that in mind, we begin to understand why the rebuilding of the temple was so vital in Haggai's day. It was the temple that would proclaim the message of the gospel that God longs to dwell with His people.

*Look back at today's passage.*
*What enabled the people to be strong?*

_____

*Why do you think the reminder of the covenant*
*promises would have encouraged the people to work?*

_____

*How can this passage encourage you in your own life?*

_____

WEEK TWO

# Haggai 2:6-9

## THE LATTER GLORY

The sovereign, covenant God will do what He has promised. He will not fail His people and His Word will stand. Immediately following the lament of the people and the encouragement from the Lord to the people for them to be strong and do the work because He is with them, we also find great encouragement. It is here that we find a promise that is rooted in the very first pages of Scripture and a constant theme of the biblical record. The glory of God will shine, and He will dwell with His people.

The promise is far-reaching and rooted in God's glory and sovereign rule over creation and His people. In fact, five times in these short verses we see the Lord addressed as the Lord of Hosts. Our God is sovereign over all from angel armies to the earth itself. Referring back to the reference of the coming of God's people out of Egypt, we are told that God will do something once more. The magnificent work of God is described for us as a shaking in the same way that we often see referred to of the Exodus events (Psalm 77:16-20). Our God and King is not finished working, but will again do great things.

We are told that these things will happen in just a little while and here the wording denotes for us not a specific time, but an urgency for which we must wait. These words are spoken from God's perspective and are on His timetable and not ours. And with Him a day is as a thousand years, and a thousand years are as a day (Psalm 90:4, 2 Peter 3:8). In an immediate sense, there would be a very near fulfillment as King Darius would provide resources for the building of God's house (Ezra 6:8), but there would be greater fulfillments to come.

Even now, we wait in expectation for the God who always keeps His promises.

As we read this passage, we cannot help but notice all of the actions that are attributed to God alone. He is instilling in the people of Haggai's day and in us as well a reminder that though He calls us to respond to Him in obedience, history is always about what God has done and not what we have done. And even the obedience with which we respond is a gracious gift of His Spirit.

This passage would see a partial fulfillment in Haggai's day, but far greater fulfillments still laid ahead. We have already seen how this theme of God's dwelling place is found from Genesis to Revelation, and we see here another example of this beautiful gospel theme. The sovereign Creator has been seeking to dwell with His people since the opening pages of Genesis. The people knew that the temple that they were building with meager resources was nowhere near as glorious and beautiful as the temple of Solomon. And yet there came a promise that something more glorious was coming. The greater glory would be found in our glorious King. Haggai is pointing us to Jesus.

Through the beauty of the incarnation, the Word became flesh and came to dwell in the midst of His people (John 1:14). And it is through Jesus that we see the greatest glory we could ever know. Jesus Himself would declare Himself to be the temple and greater than it (Matthew 12:6, John 2:19-22). God built His temple through sending His own son to be the substitutionary atonement that we so desperately needed. Even now, God is building a temple through His church, a people united to Christ through salvation. We are His living stones being build up (2 Peter 2:5, Ephesians 2:11-22, 1 Corinthians 3:9, 16-17). But still there stands a fulfillment that we await. The final glory of the temple will be seen in the consummation of all things. Creation, fall, and redemption will consummate in a glorious restoration that will return the world and the people of God to the goodness of Eden in even greater measure (Revelation 21:22-26). There in the new heavens and new earth the glory of God will shine brighter than the sun ever could. There will be no need for a physical temple because God Himself will be the temple as He dwells with His people. There the treasures of all nations will come for worship. There all will be made new (Revelation 21:5). There we will worship Him forever in perfect peace.

Read today's passage again.
Write down every action that God will do.

_____

In one sense, we already see the fulfillment
of these promises through salvation and union
with Christ. Yet, we also wait for the full and
final fulfillment of these promises. How does
this truth encourage us to live in hope?

_____

What do you learn about God in this passage?

_____

Read Revelation 21. How do you see the
promises of these verses fulfilled in the
new heavens and new earth?

_____

The final glory of this house will be greater than the first," says the Lord of Armies. "I will provide peace in this place"—this is the declaration of the Lord of Armies.

HAGGAI 2:9

# WEEKLY REFLECTION
## Week Two

## READ HAGGAI 1:9-2:9

*Paraphrase the passage from this week.*

_____

*What did you observe from this week's text about God and His character?*

_____

*What does the passage teach about the condition of mankind and about yourself?*

_____

*How does this passage point to the gospel?*

*How should you respond to this passage? What is the personal application?*

*What specific action steps can you take this week to apply the passage?*

DAY ONE

# WEEK THREE

# Haggai 2:10-14
## MAKE US CLEAN

We have come to the third oracle or sermon of the prophet Haggai. We have seen Haggai speak the Word of the Lord about the need for the temple rebuilding and for the rebuilding of God's people and their priorities in the first message. Then we saw the encouragement to the people to press on in the work that God had called them to do. Now in this third oracle, we see Haggai seek to teach the people an important lesson with rich theological truth about the blessings that come to a people who are unclean and defiled.

This sermon is preached on the day that the foundation would be laid. It had been three months since the work was begun, and two months from the encouraging message from Haggai at the beginning of chapter 2. This message is for all of the people, but Haggai begins by addressing the priests. The priests were the instructors of the law (Leviticus 10:10-11, Deuteronomy 17:9-11, Ezekiel 44:23), and Haggai had an important point to make. Of course, Haggai and the Lord knew the answer to the question that was being asked. But the point was not just to get the right answer, but to help the people understand the weight of the answer.

Haggai asked the priests about holy meat designated for offerings (Leviticus 7:14-20, Leviticus 6:25-27). The meat would be carried in the garment of the priest and would make his garment holy. But that garment could not make anything else holy. The holiness could never be transferred to the third degree. Haggai seems to be asking irrelevant questions, but we will soon see that they were very relevant. Then Haggai moves to another question. What happens if a person has become unclean by touching a dead body—do the things that they touch become unclean as well? The priests respond, yes! The uncleanness is far more contagious than the holiness. Haggai's obscure questions were asked to make an important point as he turns to the people in verse 14 and points out a greater application.

The people were weak, unclean, and dead in their sin. They had nothing to offer God. Empty religious rituals would not gain them favor with God. They needed their hearts changed. They needed to be made alive. The end of this message will declare God's blessing on this people in verse 19. Blessing was coming to an unclean and defiled people and it had nothing to do with something that they had done, but something that God had done.

This passage is full of rich truth and the theology learned here is just as needed for us today as it was for the people rebuilding the temple. God is sovereign over salvation. There is nothing that we can do to earn salvation. Ephesians 2:1-10 encapsulates this truth. We were dead in our trespasses and sins, but God in His love and mercy has made us alive. We are made clean only because of Him.

The reminder of this truth came to the people on the day the foundation was laid. This serves as a beautiful foreshadowing for us of the true foundation and cornerstone found in Jesus (1 Corinthians 3:11, 1 Peter 2:4-7). The blessing that the people experienced was an illustration of far greater spiritual blessing. Blessing comes through Jesus who is our true foundation (Ephesians 1:3, Matthew 5:3-11). Every spiritual blessing is found in Him alone.

The uncleanness of our sin has been paid for. The curse of death has been lifted. Our God is sovereign over salvation, and He has brought life where there was once only death. Our stories as the children of God echo the story of the people in Haggai's day. Our story is one of rags to riches. From the filthy rags of sin and death (Isaiah 64:6) to the righteousness of Christ and union with Him (2 Corinthians 5:21). We are made clean and made alive. We are transformed by the power of the gospel

*What are some things that people think will make them clean or righteous?*

_____

*Read Ephesians 2:1-10. How does this passage help your understanding of what it means to be made alive in Christ?*

_____

*Think about the fact that God brings life and blessing to a defiled and unclean people. Make a list of some of the attributes of God are displayed in this.*

_____

DAY TWO

# WEEK THREE

# Haggai 2:15-19
## I WILL BLESS YOU

The foundation of the temple was being laid, and it was a pivotal and important day for the people of God. God had pursued them in grace and they had repented and returned to do what He had called them to do. They were turning their backs on their apathy and walking forward in obedience. But God wanted them to pause and think about how far they had come, and all that He had done.

As people under the covenant, there were blessings promised for obedience, but there were also consequences for disobedience. These were clearly laid out throughout the Old Testament in chapters such as Deuteronomy 28. As the people, by the power of God, began to walk in covenant faithfulness, the covenant consequences would be transformed to covenant blessings.

Throughout the prophets the theme of repent and return rings out. But here God through the prophet Haggai also urges the people to remember and rejoice. As the people remembered all that God had done in changing their hearts and keeping His covenant and steadfast love, they could not help but rejoice. Grace triumphs over sin. And by His grace the vilest sinner can be made clean. The people remembered the blight, the mildew, and the hail, and these were the consequences quoted from Deuteronomy 28:22. The people had been unfaithful, but God had faithfully drawn them to Himself. We see here a shadow and a miniature new creation taking place that points to the new creation that would come with the new covenant. The old would be transformed into something new. Their paneled houses could not bring them any lasting joy and blessing, God alone could bring joy and blessing that would last forever.

After they had remembered the past, they looked around as God asked if the seed was in the barn. The passage of promised and certain blessing was declared right in the midst of the growing season. The harvest had not yet come. God promised the people something that they could not see. The fulfillment of the promise was not yet visible because the harvest season had not yet come, but that did not make the promise any less true. By faith, they had to trust that God was working deep beneath the soil. He was growing things yet unseen and fulfilling promises that were not yet visible.

Verse 19 ends with a glorious promise that from this day on, God would bless His people. In the immediate context it meant that their covenant consequences would be replaced with covenant obedience, but it also looked forward to a future and far greater blessing than they could ever imagine. The end of the book of Haggai will point us even more to this future blessing that would come in Jesus. Just as the people waited in harvest for things to grow beneath the soil that no one could see, God was working in ways that were not seen to bring about the greatest blessing. The language of chapter 19 echoes back to the covenant promises made to Abraham in Genesis 12. And these covenant promises would be fully fulfilled in Jesus Himself. Just as

a tree grows its roots beneath the ground that no one can see, God was growing the roots of His plan that was formed before the world to rescue and redeem the people that He had set His love on. It would be hundreds of years before the promise would be made visible on that first Christmas when God became a man, but deep beneath the surface, God was working.

This is how our God works. He works while we wait. He works when from the surface nothing seems to be happening. He works deep below the soil of our lives to bring about every promise. As we look back to how God worked in Haggai's day, and ultimately how He worked to bring about our Savior, we are compelled to trust Him for our lives. Just as the people of Haggai's day did, we walk forward by trusting and obeying. We may not see the harvest just yet, but He is working and growing things deep beneath the soil. And through it all we trust His sovereign hand.

*Why is it important to remember the past? How should remembering cause us to rejoice?*

_____

*How does the promise of a blessing that is not immediately seen point us to Jesus?*

_____

*As the children of God, we are always waiting for something. What are you waiting for right now, and how does this passage encourage you that God is already working?*

_____

DAY THREE

WEEK THREE

# Haggai 2:20-23

## THE CHOSEN ONE

We have come to the end of this short book, and the end of this prophecy is the promise of a new beginning. The word of the Lord came again to Haggai on the same day that the foundation of the temple was laid, and in doing so would speak of the one who would be the ultimate cornerstone (1 Peter 2:6). The promise of blessing found in verse 19 would extend so much farther than the crops of the field.

The final message of the book of Haggai is addressed to Zerubbabel the governor of Judah. It was a promise of the sovereign act of God that would overthrow kingdoms and shake the heavens and earth. The language is reminiscent of God's shaking of the earth as He brought His people out of Egypt. But what did the lowly governor of Judah and this humble servant of God have to do with the sovereign work of God?

God would in fact use Zerubbabel to help rebuild the temple, but aside from this contribution, his name seems to be nearly forgotten from the biblical story. But Zerubbabel was a shadow of another. He was pointing to a far greater fulfillment that was yet to come. He was pointing to One who would be a signet, a symbol of kingship and royal reign. He was pointing to the Servant that Isaiah also referenced. He was pointing to the One chosen before the foundation of the World (1 Peter 1:20). He was pointing to another.

In this seemingly insignificant and tiny book of Haggai, we are seeing a covenant renewal. God is reminding His people that He will not forsake the covenant that He has made with them. And the fulfillment of that covenant is totally and completely dependent on the work of His hands. Though the Davidic line and the royal signet had been taken from the expected descendant Jehoiachim (Jeremiah 22:24), it would be given to the unsuspecting governor of Judah. The covenant made to David would endure (2 Samuel 7), and God's plan would not fail.

Though the name of Zerubbabel is mentioned just a few other times in the Old Testament, and he doesn't usually top our list of most important Bible characters, his name does appear in Scripture again. On the first page of the New Testament we find his name in the genealogy of Jesus (Matthew 1:12-13). The forgotten governor's name stands with the heroes of the faith in the line of the Messiah. The chosen one, the true signet, the true servant, and the fulfillment of every promise was Jesus Himself. And Zerubbabel was chosen to point to Him.

Zerubbabel was a humble and unexpected servant that would help bring the salvation of the temple. Jesus was the humble and unexpected servant that would save His people from their sins (Matthew 1:21). Through Zerubbabel the Davidic line would be reinstated and through Jesus it would be fulfilled and established forever.

God has been faithful every step of the way and He will be faithful to the end.

*How does this passage remind you that God is sovereign over everything?*

_____

*Why do you need to be reminded of His sovereign plan?*

_____

*How does Zerubbabel point us to Jesus? What does Zerubbabel tell us about the way that God works?*

_____

DAY FOUR

# WEEK THREE

# Read
## THE ENTIRE BOOK OF HAGGAI

Summarize the message of the book
of Haggai in your own words

*(Space continued on the next page)*

Use the space below to record your own
outline of the book of Haggai

DAY FIVE

WEEK THREE

# Read

## THE ENTIRE BOOK OF HAGGAI

*As you read through the book of Haggai one last time, what themes stand out to you?*

*What single verse stands out to you as the theme verse of Haggai?*

*Write a one sentence summary of the message of Haggai.*

_____

*What have you learned about who God is and how*
*He works from the book of Haggai?*

_____

*What have you learned about how you can follow
God from the book of Haggai?*

_____

*As we close the study, write out a prayer reflecting
over what God has taught you from His Word.*

_____

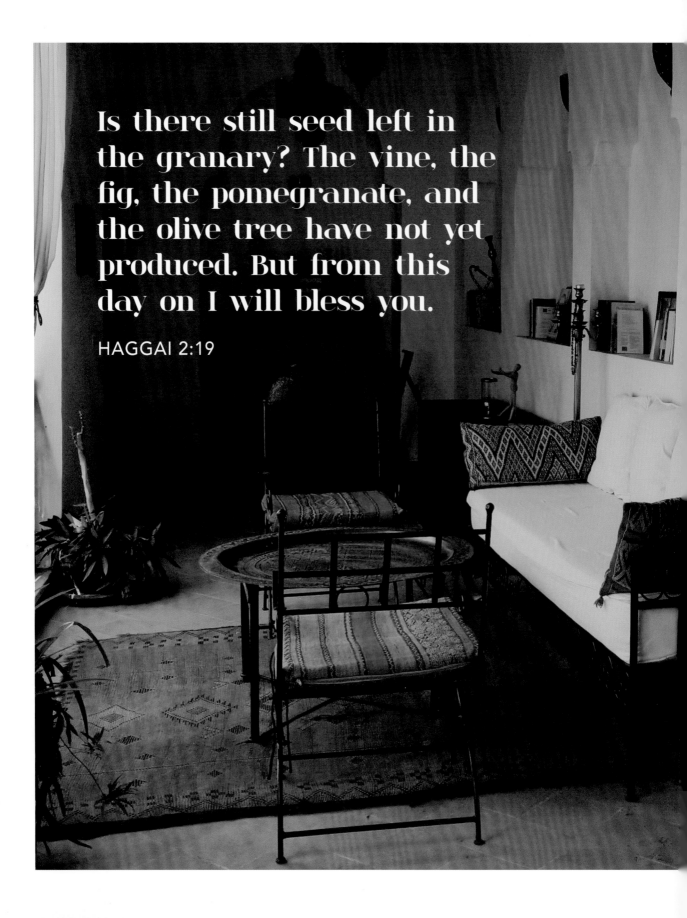

Is there still seed left in the granary? The vine, the fig, the pomegranate, and the olive tree have not yet produced. But from this day on I will bless you.

HAGGAI 2:19

## READ HAGGAI 2:10-2:23

*Paraphrase the passage from this week.*

*What did you observe from this week's text about God and His character?*

*What does the passage teach about the condition of mankind and about yourself?*

*How does this passage point to the gospel?*

_____

*How should you respond to this passage? What is the personal application?*

_____

*What specific action steps can you take this week to apply the passage?*

_____

# HAGGAI & EZRA

## CROSS REFERENCES

### HAGGAI 1:1 • EZRA 5:1

*Haggai was a prophet at the time of the reconstruction of the temple.*

### HAGGAI 1:12 • EZRA 3:8

*The people rebuilt the temple.*

### HAGGAI 1:14 • EZRA 1:1

*God rouses King Cyrus, Zerubbabel, Joshua, and the exiles to rebuild the temple.*

### HAGGAI 2:3 • EZRA 1:13

*The rebuilt temple does not look as glorious as the former temple.*

# Timeline
## OF EVENTS SURROUNDING HAGGAI

**BABYLONIAN
CAPTIVITY**

*606-536 B.C.*

**CYRUS' DEGREE**
**(2 CHRON. 36:22-23)**

*539 B.C.*

HAGGAI
ZECHERIAH

**TEMPLE WORK
RESUMED**

*520 B.C.*

**TEMPLE FINISHED**

*516 B.C.*

EZRA
NEHEMIAH

# Characters

## IN HAGGAI 1:1

### KING DARIUS

Pagan ruler over the Persian Empire from 522-486 BC.

### ZERUBBABEL

Grandson of Judah's King Jehoiachin, the ruler at the time of Judah's exile. This places him in the Davidic line of kingship. During the exile, Persia appointed him as governor of the people of Judah.

### SHEALTIEL

Father of Zerubbabel and son of King Jehoiachin.

### JOSHUA

High Priest in post-exilic Judah, following in his father's footsteps.

### JEHOZADAK

Father of Joshua, high priest over Judah at the time of the Exile.

In the second year of King Darius, on the first day of the sixth month, the word of the Lord came through the prophet Haggai to Zerubbabel son of Shealtiel, the governor of Judah, and to Joshua son of Jehozadak, the high priest

*Haggai 1:1*

# THE GLORY OF GOD
## AND THE TEMPLE

The Tabernacle is built, and the glory of God fills it.
### —— EXODUS 40:34 ——

The Temple is built, and the glory of God fills it.
### —— 2 CHRONICLES 5:13-14 ——

The glory of God leaves the Temple at Judah's exile.
### —— EZEKIEL 10 ——

Ezekiel prophecies that the glory of God will
eventually return and bring restoration.
### —— EZEKIEL 43 ——

The glory of the Lord does not return
to the Temple once it is rebuilt.
### —— HAGGAI 2:1-9 ——

John sees that there is no need for a physical temple
in the New Creation; the temple is God.
### —— REVELATION 21:22 ——

# What is the gospel?

Thank you for reading and enjoying this study with us! We are abundantly grateful for the Word of God, the instruction we glean from it, and the ever-growing understanding about God's character from it. We're also thankful that Scripture continually points to one thing in innumerable ways: the gospel.

We remember our brokenness when we read about the fall of Adam and Eve in the garden of Eden (Genesis 3), when sin entered into a perfect world and maimed it. We remember the necessity that something innocent must die to pay for our sin when we read about the atoning sacrifices in the Old Testament. We read that we have all sinned and fallen short of the glory of God (Romans 3:23), and that the penalty for our brokenness, the wages of our sin, is death (Romans 6:23). We all are in need of grace, mercy, and most importantly—we all need a Savior.

We consider the goodness of God when we realize that He did not plan to leave us in this dire state. We see His promise to buy us back from the clutches of sin and death in Genesis 3:15. And we see that promise accomplished with Jesus Christ on the cross. Jesus Christ knew no sin yet became sin so that we might become righteous through His sacrifice (2 Corinthians 5:21.) Jesus was tempted in every way that we are and lived sinlessly. He was reviled, yet still yielded Himself for our sake, that we may have life abundant in Him. Jesus lived the perfect life that we could not live and died the death that we deserved.

The gospel is profound yet simple. There are many mysteries in it that we can never exhaust this side of heaven, but there is still overwhelming weight to its implications in this life. The gospel is the telling of our sinfulness and God's goodness, and this gracious gift compels a response. We are saved by grace through faith (Ephesians 2:8-9), which means that we rest with faith in the grace that Jesus Christ displayed on the cross. We cannot save ourselves from our brokenness or do any amount of good works to merit God's favor, but we can have faith that what Jesus accomplished in His death, burial, and resurrection was more than enough for our salvation and our eternal delight. When we accept God, we are commanded to die to our self and our sinful desires and live a life worthy of the calling we have received (Ephesians 4:1). The gospel compels us to be sanctified, and in so doing, we are conformed to the likeness of Christ Himself.

This is hope. This is redemption. This is the gospel.

He made the one who did not know sin to be sin for us, so that in him we might become the righteousness of God.

2 CORINTHIANS 5:21

# THANK YOU

FOR STUDYING GOD'S
WORD WITH US!

**CONNECT WITH US:**

@THEDAILYGRACECO

@KRISTINSCHMUCKER

**CONTACT US:**

INFO@THEDAILYGRACECO.COM

**SHARE:**

#THEDAILYGRACECO

#LAMPANDLIGHT

**WEBSITE:**

WWW.THEDAILYGRACECO.COM

———